What Item Would You Put into a Time Capsule?

by Mrs. Chavez-Huynh's class
with Tony Stead

capstone®
classroom

What is a time capsule? It's a bottle or box or trunk in which you can put your most precious or important objects. In the future you can reopen it and be reminded of the memories, events, and moments of your life. Opening a time capsule can also teach us about important times in history. Many cities bury time capsules to show future generations what the city was like. Individuals can save important items too!

In this book eight of us share what we would put in a time capsule and explain why these things are the **best** items for a time capsule. These objects vary from dresses to bears to photographs. Read about our special time capsules, and think about what you would put in yours if you were given the opportunity.

TIME
CAPSULE

Family Photos

If I could put any item into a time capsule, I would choose my family pictures. They would remind me of all the fun things I did with my family and friends, all the journeys I took with them, and the important memories that we made.

Why are these pictures so important? When I spend time with my family and friends, I feel great because I get to visit them. When I go to their homes, I feel joy because they are all there, and I love them so much. Sometimes I invite cousins to my house. My favorite time to visit is the summer because I can stay with them longer since I don't need to go to school.

The pictures hold special memories. For instance, one time I went to a fair with my family. We had a great time on the rides and playing games, and I will never forget that day. Another memory I have from those pictures is of a game we used to play called *Las Escondidas*. It's a really fun game. Sometimes I show my friends how to play too.

My pictures are so important to me. What's more important than remembering good times you've had with your family? That's why family photographs are the single most important item to put in a time capsule. Those photographs hold so many amazing memories.

by Maria

My Teddy Bear!

He's soft, he's cuddly, and he reminds me of good times from my childhood. Who is he? He's my teddy bear! And he's the most important item to put into a time capsule because he will help me remember all the adventures that I had when I was little.

This teddy bear reminds me of my childhood. When I was in Mexico, my mom bought me the teddy bear at the fair. I used to play with my bear, my cousins Juana and Perla, and my Aunt Monica. I carried the bear around so much that sometimes it fell in the mud! My grandmother would always wash it when I was sleeping so that I didn't know the bear was away from me. If I ran through the sprinkler with my cousin Juana, I took the bear too. He always dried out in the sun.

My teddy bear and I had a lot of adventures at the fair, at the store—everywhere! He played games with me, and I dressed him. I pretended to feed him at dinnertime, and I even took him on a horseback ride! Just holding the bear brings back a flood of amazing memories. This object is the most important thing from my childhood, and that's why the teddy bear belongs in a time capsule. Think about the most important object that you have! Would you put it in a capsule to remember it forever?

by Mayte

My Favorite Game

If I could put any item into a time capsule, I'd choose my favorite game—my battling character cards. I remember how I showed my healing cards and battling cards to my family and the battles I had with my friends.

I remember when I first got the cards and showed them to my family. They were a little interested, but once they started playing, they were VERY interested! I was happy and excited because my family would play cards with me. These cards created special memories of when my parents were excited and happy—and I was too.

I used the cards to battle with my friends. I'd say, "Let's have one battle." But hours later, we'd still be battling, trying to figure out who was the best at the game. It didn't matter, though—we were just having fun.

Photographs are great, and there are many ways to remember the good times you had when you were a kid. But these cards helped me have amazing times with my friends. We'd get together and play and have so much fun. That's why these cards are the most important item to put into a time capsule! But first ... one more game!

by Eduardo

My Special Dress

When I was a baby, my family had an important ceremony for me. I wore a beautiful dress for this occasion, and this dress reminds me of a time that was special for my family. Because this event was so meaningful, the dress is the most important item I have to go into a time capsule.

Why is this dress so important? It came from my mom and my grandparents. They gathered money to buy the most beautiful dress they could afford, and they were very proud when they saw how beautiful I looked. My whole family was there for the celebration, and everyone couldn't wait to be part of this special time with a new baby in the family. That baby was me, and my family has been close to me ever since then. I heard that I cried a lot at this celebration because I was so little and got very tired. But I slept while my family had a party! My parents, brothers, aunts, uncles, cousins, and friends all celebrated. Now that I am older, I have been to a few of these celebrations, and I know how special they are.

Even though I can't remember the ceremony, I know it was an important part of my life. The dress is the most important item to put into the time capsule because the fabric of the dress is like the fabric that holds my family together. The dress reminds me that family is strong and important. I am very lucky to have my family, and that's the best thing to remember!

by Jessica

Family Videos

To me, nothing is more important than family. That is why I would choose to put videos of my family in a time capsule. There are videos in particular I would choose—videos of my grandparents. Why are these so special? Because I have never met my grandparents. They died before I was born.

Through the videos, my grandparents come to life for me. I love them so much because I've been able to see them. The videos show where they lived and how they lived. I got to see the house where my parents lived with my grandma when my parents were first married—before they had me. I saw my grandma's kitchen, where she cooked amazing meals for the family, and the garden, where my grandpa grew all the fresh vegetables that grandma used to cook. They were loving and caring people, and I would not know them if there were not videos of them.

The videos are the most important thing to put into the time capsule because they teach me about my past. Without them, I would never know these special people. So that's why I chose these videos over all the other items from my childhood. Who would you like to remember the most? Make a video and save it for the future before it's too late!

by Alicia

My Diary

It holds my feelings, my happiness, my secrets, and the things that have happened in my life. What is it? It's my diary, and it's the most important item that I would put in a time capsule. My diary represents my life the best.

I can imagine digging up this time capsule in the future and finding a quiet spot under a tree to read my old diary. I'd remember my early school days, the best holidays I ever had, and times with my family. In addition, I would remember my birthdays, my school friends, and what it was like to be with my grandparents. It would be great to relive my happy times, to reread all my old secrets, and even to remember the sad times because I learned from them. My diary would be full of accomplishments. Of course I'd want to remember all of this!

The diary wouldn't be wonderful just for me, but also for future members of my family who may not get the chance to meet me. The diary would let them know about my life, just like my grandma's diary lets me know about her life. The diary would give hope to my family in the future.

When I thumb through the pages of my diary, I remember trips with my family. I remember going to Galveston and to Mexico to see my relatives. I can relive times that were both happy and sad. Saving these memories is very important. That's why my diary would go into the time capsule to save forever.

by Clariza

Photographs Hold the Past

Right now, my friends are very important to me! But I can't put my friends into a time capsule. I can, though, put photos of my friends into a time capsule. I can't think of anything more important to save for the future. These photographs will remind me of how young I was, the special friends I had, and the fun things we did. And when I look at the backgrounds of the photographs, I'll see how everything looked a long time ago. What a great way to remember the past!

My friends are John, Ani, Luis, and Angel. We have so much fun on field trips, at birthday parties, and just hanging out at each other's houses and playing together. What if I lost touch with these friends later in my life? I'd always have the pictures to remind me of them and the good times we shared.

These photos help me remember important people too! My music teacher and my PE teacher have been very important to me. I love music and I love sports, and I know when I see these pictures, they will remind me of these special people and what they taught me. I had so much fun in their classes. I want to be sure I never forget! My family is important too. This picture of my brother and sister reminds me of a contest we had. Another picture shows a trip to the water park and the first time my little brother was brave enough to go on the slide. I want to be sure to always remember these special times.

My photographs have old things in them, like old-fashioned phones and computers. In the future I bet these things will look really funny. I'll want to share them with my own kids someday! They will wonder where we got these antiques.

Photographs hold so many special memories. That's why they are the most important things to put in a time capsule!

by Aldo

Remembering a Family Party

My family had a magical day, a day that took a lot of planning and organizing, but a day that I will always remember. I want to save photos of this family day because it was a special time with my family and friends. The work that went into planning it was almost as fun as the event itself! I want to remember it forever, and that's why these photographs should be the first things in the time capsule.

I can picture the day so clearly in my mind—the big, brown building where we traveled to, the noise of my large family getting louder and louder as more people came, the photographer flashing his bulb and making me blink, special gifts from my family, the delicious pizza we had afterward. When we got home, we had a big cake waiting for us and lots of friends too! As the day continued, a bounce house showed up on the front lawn. I will never forget how fun it was to bounce inside it and celebrate with my friends, the looks of joy

on our faces, and the silly stunts that we did. When we got out of the bounce house, more food was waiting. My mom's mole sauce was perfect! We ate tamales and rice until we were stuffed. And we have pictures that show each part of that special day.

To conclude, I always will remember this wonderful celebration through my photos. I think about opening the time capsule 50 years from now and smiling and laughing with my own children when I share these photos. And that's what makes family so special and why I want to be sure that I remember all these special times. A time capsule is the perfect safe place to store my photographs.

by Rocio

A time capsule would be a great way to preserve the past and remember the important things that happened in our lives. But it would be hard to choose just one thing to put into a time capsule—so many things are important! Family photographs, videos, games, diaries, and toys can all help us remember special times. What would you put into a time capsule of your own? What makes that the **best** thing to put into your time capsule?